8.12a Grant 2006
Wed - Fred

10/10/05 Penworthy $22.60

CROSS-SECTIONS

THE F/A-22
RAPTOR

by Ole Steen Hansen
illustrated by Alex Pang
Consultant: Craig Hoyle, Defense Editor, Flight International

Capstone
press
Mankato, Minnesota

First published in the United States in 2006 by Capstone Press
151 Good Counsel Drive, P.O. Box 669, Mankato, Minnesota 56002
http://www.capstonepress.com

Library of Congress Cataloging-in-Publication Data
Hansen, Ole Steen.
     The F/A-22 Raptor / by Ole Steen Hansen.
     p. cm.—(Edge books, cross-sections)
     Summary: "An in-depth look at the F/A-22 Raptor, with detailed cross-section
diagrams, action photos, and fascinating facts"—Provided by publisher.
     Includes bibliographical references and index.
     ISBN 0-7368-5253-0 (hardcover)
     1. F/A-22 (Jet fighter plane)—Juvenile literature. 2. Fighter planes—United
States—Juvenile literature. I. Pang, Alex, ill. II. Title.
UG1242.F5H358 2006
623.74'64—dc22   2005009641

Designed and produced by

David West ᨆᨆ Children's Books
7 Princeton Court
55 Felsham Road
Purney
London SW15 1AZ

Designer: Gary Jeffrey
Editors: Gail Bushnell, Kate Newport

Photo Credits
U.S. Airforce photo, 14, 15, 16, 19, 23, 25; U.S. Airforce photo by tech sgt. Kevin J
Gruenwald, 6-7, 11b, 22; U.S. Airforce photo by staff sgt. Tia Schroder, 10; U.S.
Airforce photo by John Rossino, 11t; U.S. Airforce photo by 2nd lt. Albert Bosco, 13,
24; U.S. Airforce photo by Ken Hackman, 18; U.S. Airforce photo by master sgt.
Mike Ammons; U.S. Airforce photo by Kevin Robertson; U.S. Navy photo by
intelligence specialist 1st class Kenneth Moll, 20; Nasa Dryden Flight Research Center,
6c; Nasa Dryden Flight Research Center, Jim Ross 6b

1 2 3 4 5 6 10 09 08 07 06 05

TABLE OF CONTENTS

THE F/A-22 RAPTOR

Fighter aircraft are designed to shoot down enemy aircraft. The well-armed jets must be fast and easy to maneuver. The U.S. Air Force is developing the F/A-22 Raptor. This fighter will be the most effective fighter ever flown. It won't just be able to attack aircraft. It will also attack ground targets.

Here, an F/A-22 Raptor flies above an F-16. In the 1980s, the F-16 was one of the top fighters in the world. Today, the F-16 is used mostly to drop bombs. The Raptor is both a fighter and a bomber.

SUPER-FIGHTERS

To win battles in the sky, fighter pilots must be highly trained. They must also have the best aircraft.

WORLD WAR II

During World War II (1939–1945), Allied forces fought great air battles over Germany. Allied fighters destroyed the German Air Force and helped win the war. In the Pacific, U.S. fighters fought Japanese aircraft and ships. P-38 Lightning fighters shot down more Japanese aircraft than any other type of U.S. fighter.

With its twin tail booms, the P-38 looked like no other fighter.

During World War II, the P-51 Mustang had the range to fly deep into Germany and destroy German Air Force planes.

The Russian Su-27 Flanker is still among the most maneuverable and heavily armed fighters in the world.

COLD WAR

During the Cold War, the United States and the Soviet Union both wanted superior aircraft. When the Soviet Su-27 Flanker became a threat, the U.S. Air Force designed the F/A-22 Raptor. The Raptor will ensure that the United States will have the best fighter.

The F-15 was the most up-to-date western Cold War fighter. F-15s are still flying with the U.S. Air Force today.

CROSS-SECTION

It has taken more than 20 years to develop the F/A-22 Raptor.

The Raptor will be a stealthy fighter. No other aircraft will be able to fly at higher speeds while being so difficult for the enemy to find.

The labels show where you can find more information about the features of a Raptor.

Lt Col. Gary Jeffrey

COCKPIT
See pages 16–17

AVIONICS
See pages 20–21

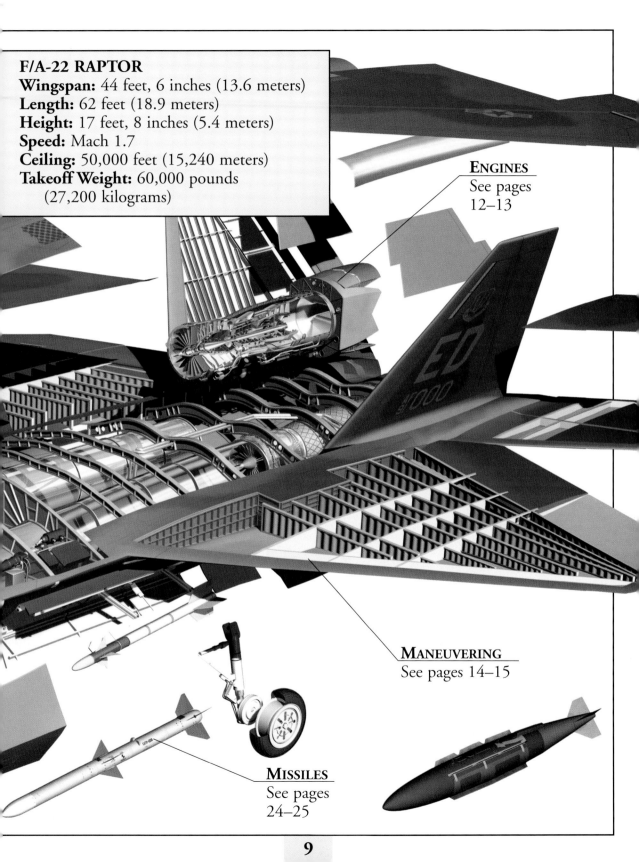

F/A-22 RAPTOR
Wingspan: 44 feet, 6 inches (13.6 meters)
Length: 62 feet (18.9 meters)
Height: 17 feet, 8 inches (5.4 meters)
Speed: Mach 1.7
Ceiling: 50,000 feet (15,240 meters)
Takeoff Weight: 60,000 pounds
     (27,200 kilograms)

ENGINES
See pages
12–13

MANEUVERING
See pages 14–15

MISSILES
See pages
24–25

STEALTH

A stealth aircraft is difficult for the enemy to detect with radar or with the naked eye. The Raptor is the first fighter plane designed to be stealthy.

Radar works by sending out waves that are then reflected back by any objects they hit. Enemy radar will have great difficulty detecting the Raptor. Radar waves scatter as they hit the streamlined Raptor. W-shaped edges and the angle of the wings, tail, and air intake are designed to scatter radar waves.

CAMOUFLAGE PAINT

W-SHAPED EDGES

The B-2 bomber was the first stealth aircraft to have rounded shapes made with composite materials. These different materials are blended so that the most important parts of each can be used. This technology is also used on the Raptor.

ANGLES OF WING
AND TAIL ARE
DESIGNED TO
SCATTER RADAR.

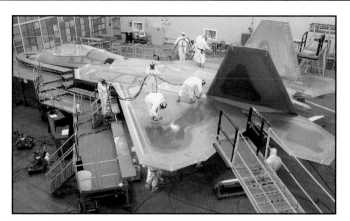

FLUSH PANELS

The paint used on the Raptor absorbs some radar waves. The colors make the aircraft difficult to see with the naked eye.

SWEPT BACK AIR
INTAKE EDGES

Angles on leading edges of the wings, tail, and air intake help keep the Raptor hidden.

Radar waves need to bounce off a flat surface. The Raptor has no flat surfaces.

The panels on the Raptor must be built completely flush with the surface. Any edge sticking out can be seen on enemy radar.

THE ENGINES

The Raptor has the most powerful jet engines ever developed for a fighter plane. The exhaust nozzles can be turned to help maneuver the aircraft.

Most fighters need afterburners to fly supersonic, which is faster than the speed of sound. Afterburners use up fuel quickly, so the planes can fly only for a short time. The F/A-22 Raptor can fly faster than the speed of sound for long periods. It does not need the afterburner to fly at supersonic speeds.

ENGINE SPECIFICATIONS
Two Pratt and Whitney F119-PW-100 engines, each producing 35,000 lbs of (15,900 kilograms) of thrust.

The Raptor engines have almost the same power as engines on a Boeing 757 airliner with 200 seats.

COMBUSTION CHAMBER
Fuel is burned here with the compressed air.

COMPRESSOR
The compressor blades turn at high speeds and compress the air.

AIR INTAKE
Large fans at the front of the engine suck in air.

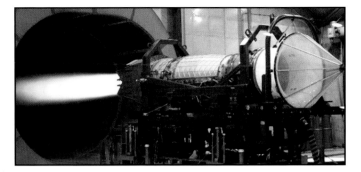

The exhaust nozzles can move 20 degrees up and down. This movement changes the direction of the exhaust to help maneuver the Raptor.

Using the afterburner provides extra thrust and speed. The afterburner also produces extra heat that can attract enemy heat-seeking missiles. This afterburner (*above*) is being tested on the ground.

Afterburner

Fuel is injected into the exhaust gases to produce extra power. This feature uses a lot of fuel and is very noisy, but it allows the plane to fly at supersonic speeds.

Position of jet engines on Raptor

MANEUVERING

The F/A-22 Raptor handles extremely well. Many F/A-22 pilots say it is one of the best machines to fly.

Pilots control the Raptor using the same equipment as most other aircraft. When the pilot moves the stick and pedals in the cockpit, signals go to a computer. The computer then determines how to move the controls most efficiently. This is called a fly-by-wire system.

The Raptor is a big fighter, but it can still turn and maneuver effectively in close combat.

RUDDER

AILERON (OUTER CONTROL SURFACE ON WING TRAILING EDGE)

LEADING-EDGE FLAPS

The computer combines the movements of controls and flaps. It makes sure that the Raptor does not fly beyond its limits.

ALL MOVING TAILPLANE (ELEVATOR)

FLAPERON – COMBINED FLAPS AND AILERON (INNER CONTROL SURFACE ON WING TRAILING EDGE)

An aircraft loses speed when it turns suddenly. The powerful engines of the Raptor make it possible for the fighter to maintain high speeds even when turning.

The Raptor takes less than a second to turn. See below.

3. The Raptor banks using ailerons. The flaperons, elevator, and turned exhaust nozzle help to sustain the turn.

2. The elevator and exhaust nozzle move up to press down the tail. The flaperon moves down to create more lift on the wing.

1. This Raptor must turn while climbing in close combat.

THE COCKPIT

The Raptor cockpit is designed to help the pilot fly the aircraft and be aware of activity across huge distances.

Computers help the pilot to navigate and fly the fighter. They also help the pilot locate friends and enemies, as well as select and fire the appropriate weapons. All of this information is shown on computer displays in the cockpit.

KEY TO DIAGRAM
1. Sidestick controller
2. Engine throttles
3. Ejector seat firing handle
4. Head-up display (HUD)
5–7. Displays giving vital information on speed, altitude and targets
8. Main display for navigating and fighting
9–10. Displays mainly giving information on weapons, emergencies, fuel, and enemy radar

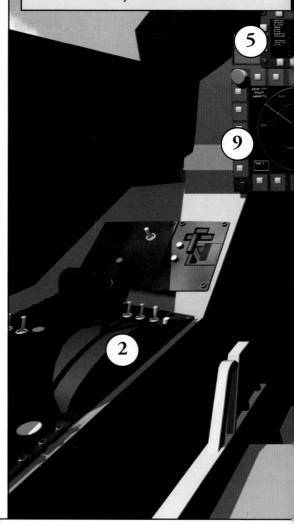

On the head-up display (HUD), the pilot can access information on speed, altitude, and targets while still being able to look out of the cockpit.

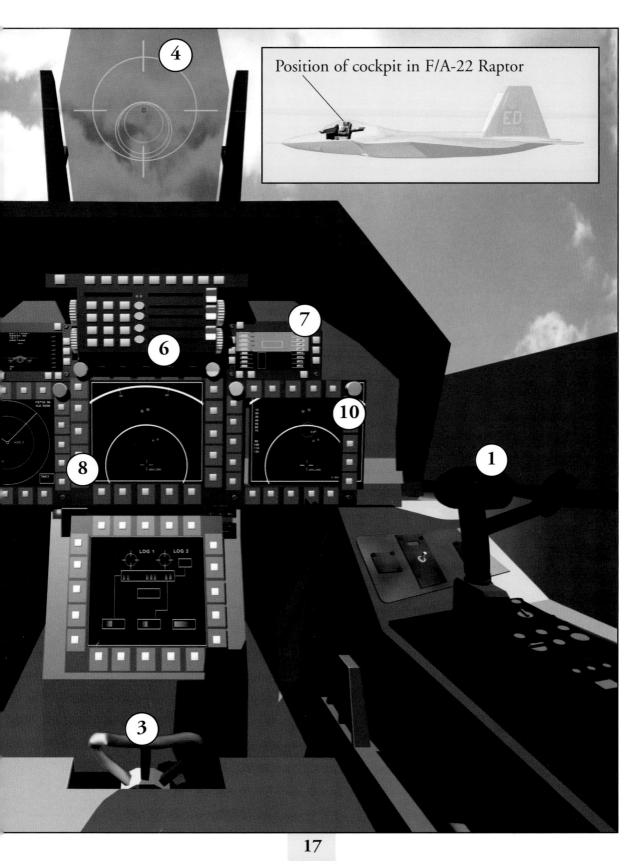

Position of cockpit in F/A-22 Raptor

PILOT

Even with the computers in the F/A-22 Raptor, a pilot is still needed. The human brain is better than a computer when it comes to making vital decisions.

In the cockpit before takeoff. Once in the air, the pilot needs to fly, fight, and think fast at all times.

In a sharp turn, a pilot may be subjected to 9 g-forces. Pilots can feel like they weigh up to nine times their actual weight. Under this pressure, blood drains from the brain, which can cause the pilot to faint. To keep the blood in the upper part of the body, pilots wear G suits. When g-forces build up, the G suit fills with air and presses on the pilot's legs, so blood cannot easily be forced down into them. This pressure then keeps the blood from leaving the brain.

AS THE TURN TIGHTENS, THE G-FORCES CAN BUILD UP FROM 3 GS TO 9 GS. 9 GS IS THE MOST THE RAPTOR'S COMPUTER CAN HANDLE.

9 Gs

6 Gs

3 Gs

1 G

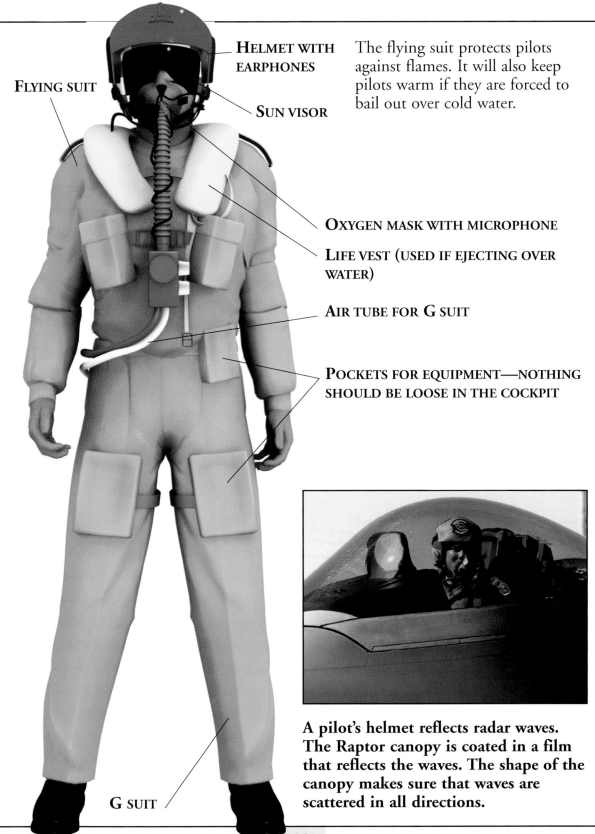

HELMET WITH EARPHONES

FLYING SUIT

SUN VISOR

The flying suit protects pilots against flames. It will also keep pilots warm if they are forced to bail out over cold water.

OXYGEN MASK WITH MICROPHONE

LIFE VEST (USED IF EJECTING OVER WATER)

AIR TUBE FOR G SUIT

POCKETS FOR EQUIPMENT—NOTHING SHOULD BE LOOSE IN THE COCKPIT

G SUIT

A pilot's helmet reflects radar waves. The Raptor canopy is coated in a film that reflects the waves. The shape of the canopy makes sure that waves are scattered in all directions.

AVIONICS

Electronics in an aircraft are called avionics. The avionics in the Raptor help the pilot find the enemy and keep in contact with friendly aircraft.

The Raptor uses its radar to find enemy aircraft. The radar warning receivers tell the pilot if enemy radar is looking for aircraft. The pilot also uses the datalink antenna to keep in touch with friendly aircraft.

Position of main avionics on F/A-22 Raptor

RADAR WARNING RECEIVERS

RADAR WARNING RECEIVERS

AN/AGP-77 RADAR

DATALINK ANTENNA

The AN/APG-77 radar
This radar system is made of 2,000 small modules that both transmit and receive signals. The radar can handle many jobs at the same time.

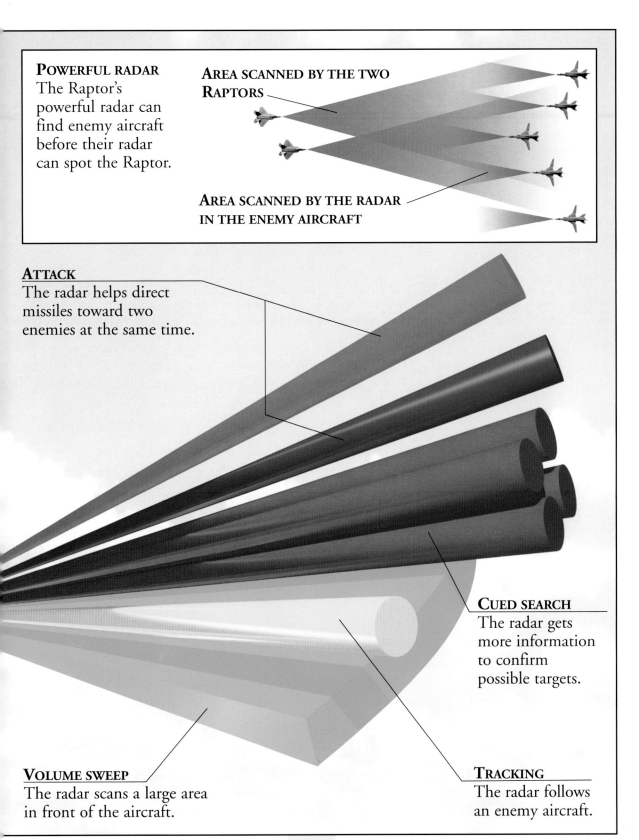

POWERFUL RADAR
The Raptor's powerful radar can find enemy aircraft before their radar can spot the Raptor.

AREA SCANNED BY THE TWO RAPTORS

AREA SCANNED BY THE RADAR IN THE ENEMY AIRCRAFT

ATTACK
The radar helps direct missiles toward two enemies at the same time.

CUED SEARCH
The radar gets more information to confirm possible targets.

VOLUME SWEEP
The radar scans a large area in front of the aircraft.

TRACKING
The radar follows an enemy aircraft.

WEAPONS

The F/A-22 Raptor carries missiles to shoot down enemy aircraft and bombs to hit targets on the ground.

Most military aircraft have bombs or missiles hanging under the wings or fuselage. The Raptor usually carries all its weapons in internal weapon bays. Bombs or missiles hanging under the wings would make the Raptor show up on enemy radar.

The Raptor has four hard points under the wing where bombs or missiles can be hung. Usually the Raptor will fly with the weapons inside to preserve its stealth qualities.

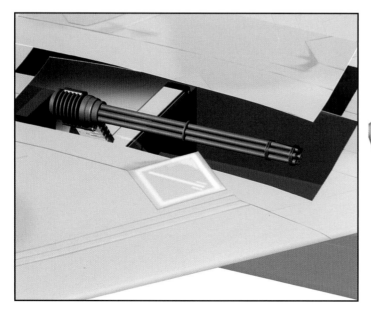

For very close combat, the Raptor has a six-barrel machine gun placed over the right air intake. It fires hundreds of rounds per second.

With the weapons carried inside the aircraft, the Raptor has less drag, or resistance to the air. It can fly longer and faster.

KEY TO WEAPONS
1. AIM-120 AMRAAM (air-to-air missile)
2. AIM-9 Sidewinder (air-to-air missile)
3. GBU-32 JDAM (GPS directed bomb)

2

3

1

MISSILES

A Raptor pilot's aim is to shoot down enemy aircraft at long range. Sometimes this must take place before the enemy is in sight.

Long-range fighting is called "beyond visual range." The Raptor has a long-range radar. It can detect the enemy before the enemy has detected the Raptor. The pilot then uses AIM-120 missiles to shoot down the enemy at long range.

TEST FIRING OF A SIDEWINDER
Pilots always try to avoid fighting at close range, but it can become necessary. In these situations, the pilot uses the Sidewinder missile.

ROCKET MOTOR

CONTROL FINS

PROPELLANT

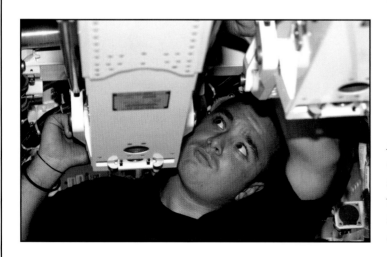

A modern fighter has many electronics to maintain and adjust. The missiles must work together with the aircraft's radar and target computer.

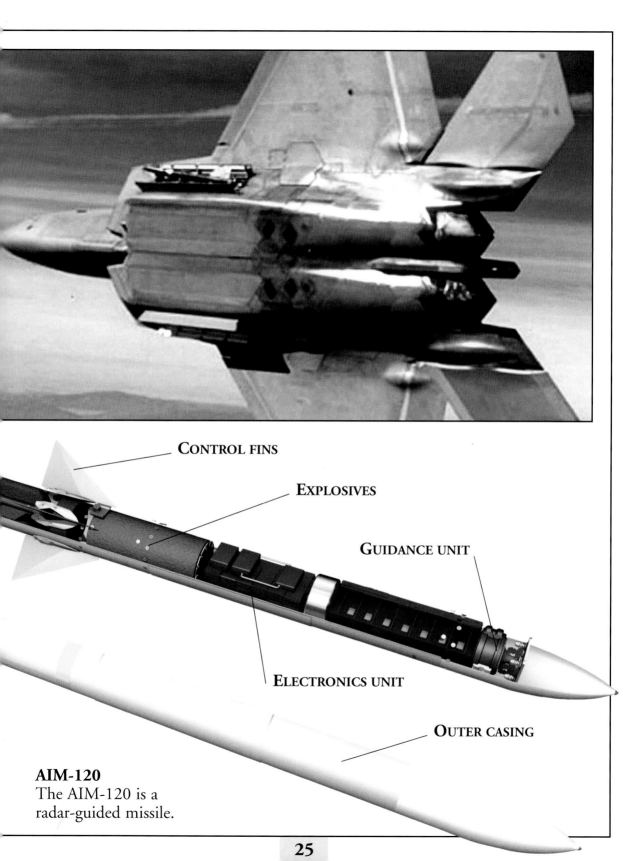

CONTROL FINS

EXPLOSIVES

GUIDANCE UNIT

ELECTRONICS UNIT

OUTER CASING

AIM-120
The AIM-120 is a
radar-guided missile.

THE MISSION

The F/A-22 Raptor is designed to be used for many kinds of missions. Its tasks include escorting bombers to their targets and destroying enemy attackers.

Here, two Raptors are being sent out to destroy an attacker. They use a combination of stealth, radar, datalink, and missiles to find and then shoot down the enemy. The pilot only needs to see the enemy as a dot on the radar screen.

1. Two Raptors take off and fly toward the enemy in a loose formation. Only one of the Raptors has its radar switched on.

5. The enemy registers the missile and tries to take evasive action, but it is too late.

4. The Raptor can't be detected by radar. It gets into missile firing range and launches an AIM-120 against the enemy plane. The enemy has no idea it is there.

3. The radar warning receiver on this enemy plane tells the pilot a radar is scanning his plane. Because the Raptor is stealthy, the pilot cannot actually see it on his own radar.

2. The enemy aircraft is spotted on radar. The Raptor relays this radar image to the other Raptor via datalink. Even though the three aircraft cannot see one another, the Raptor pilots know where everybody is.

THE FUTURE

The Raptor was designed to counter threats from high-tech fighter aircraft. The end of the Cold War means that this is no longer the biggest threat to the U.S. Air Force.

Today, terrorism is the biggest threat to U.S. security. The Raptor is not designed for these types of threats. However, no one knows what the future holds. As the world's best fighter, the Raptor will always be valuable to the U.S. Air Force.

Shown here are some other types of fighter craft and weapons.

Cruise missiles hit their targets with great precision. They don't need an escort.

The Raptor is an effective fighter, but it is expensive to build and maintain. The F-35 Joint Strike Fighter (*above*) is less effective but much cheaper.

A formation of five
F-15 Eagles followed by
an F/A-22 Raptor—
the fighter that will
replace them in the
U.S. Air Force.

The ultimate in fighter
design. A formation of
four Raptors.

GLOSSARY

afterburner (AF-tur-bur-nur)—the part of a jet engine that burns extra fuel with the exhaust gases to produce extra thrust

aileron (AY-luh-ron)—a flap on the back of the wing which helps the aircraft balance

avionics (ay-vee-ON-iks)—the electronics in an aircraft

composite materials (kuhm-POZ-it muh-TIHR-ee-uhls)—a special mixture of materials for superior performance

exhaust (eg-ZAWST)—heated air leaving a jet engine

fuselage (FYOO-suh-lahzh)—the main part of a plane where the crew or passengers sit

radar (RAY-dar)—equipment that uses radio waves to find or guide objects

Sidewinder missile (SIDE-winde-er MISS-uhl)—a missile that finds its target by the heat the target gives off

supersonic (soo-pur-SON-ik)—faster than the speed of sound

thrust (THRUHST)—the force that pushes an aircraft forward